Hope, A Myth Reawakened

"Lillian Moats aspires to reawaken in us a sense of hope in an age dominated by confusion, trepidation and despair. Her allegory seduces readers into serious reflections on the nature and sources of hope. The language herein is inviting, the insights are abundant, and the suspense is captivating. Perhaps you will detect, as I did, hints of Dante and Plato as the author engages Hope and Despair in constructive dialogue. This book is inspiring, and you are to be envied if you can find something better to do than to read it."

—*Loyal Rue*, Emeritus Professor of Philosophy
and Religion, Luther College

The Letter from Death

". . . In her fourth book, Moats performs an astonishing feat. By imagining Death as a patient and suffering entity fluent in human affairs, she broaches matters of daunting complexity with galvanizing directness. . . . this clarion critique offers an arresting perspective on religion, our "growing militarism," our "inexhaustible genius for denial," and our paradoxical failure to nurture our best qualities. . . . Moats has created a wise, unsettling, and beautiful book."

—*Donna Seaman*, BOOKLIST, July 1, 2009

Legacy of Shadows

"This book will hold its readers close and tight, will teach them its remarkable, affecting and important lesson: that experiences live and last over a family's generations as memories that shape hearts and minds."

—*Robert Coles, M.D.*, Research Psychiatrist,
Harvard University Health Services.
Pulitzer Prize-winning author of *The Moral Life of Children*.

The Gate of Dreams

"The stories have a pleasing old-fashioned mood, which is accented by the exquisite illustrations . . . dainty, beautifully proportioned, finely detailed silhouettes done in black on white and scattered across the pages; at any moment they seem ready to leap into action." —SCHOOL LIBRARY JOURNAL

IF YOU EXIST

IN SEARCH OF A READER
DEEP IN THE FUTURE

Lillian Moats

IF YOU EXIST

IN SEARCH OF A READER
DEEP IN THE FUTURE

Lillian Moats

Three Arts Press
DOWNERS GROVE, ILLINOIS

THREE ARTS PRESS
1100 Maple Ave
Downers Grove, IL 60515-4818

Text © 2021
Cover design by Lillian, David & Michael Moats
Book design by Sarah Miner
Author photo by Marlayna Schoen
Printed in the United States on acid-free paper by Bookmobile

Published 2021 by Three Arts Press.

Library of Congress Control Number: 2021905381

PUBLISHER'S CATALOGING-IN-PUBLICATION DATA

Names: Moats, Lillian, author.
Title: If you exist : in search of a reader deep in the future / Lillian Moats.
Description: Downers Grove, IL : Three Arts Press, 2021. | Includes bibliographical references.
Identifiers: ISBN 9781736723203 (paperback) | ISBN 9781736723210 (ebook)
Subjects: LCSH: Future, The. | Human beings—Forecasting. | Earth (Planet)—Forecasting. | Extinction (Biology) | Social problems—Forecasting. | Technology—Moral and ethical aspects. | BISAC: PHILOSOPHY / Essays. | SOCIAL SCIENCE / Essays. | LCGFT: Essays.
Classification: LCC PS3569.O6523 I4 2021 (print) | LCC PS3569.O6523 (ebook) | DDC 814/.54—dc23

For Michael,
Dave and Jen

and remembering "Pen"

TABLE OF CONTENTS

Preface *xi*

PREFACE

October, 2020

Welcome to this little book you never expected to be reading, nor whose author I expected to be. The last several years have brought on, or at least heightened, my "existential depression" which I think has become common among feeling people and is growing more so, though perhaps most people who experience it do not know it by that name.

In recent years meanness has replaced civility and common purpose; in recent months, isolation and heightened awareness of racial and class inequities have been spotlighted by the COVID-19 pandemic. These have elicited in many of us a heartsick feeling upon waking or an inability to sleep. With every broadcast of news, with every new topical book consumed may come a growing anxiety about the future of our planet.

Looking existential issues in the eye, rather than letting them swirl and spiral in my mind has helped with my depression. It is the same sort of lesson one learns in therapy. Bringing despair into the light can disarm the darkness. I would be gratified if reading *If You Exist* could help you, too.

Lillian Moats

IF YOU EXIST

1

IF YOU EXIST, 2009

I WRITE THIS OUT OF A KIND OF NERVOUSNESS, not really to be heard by anyone living now. There is such a din of voices, such disguised panic in the present.

And so I write to you who may not even exist, to human progeny—mine or anyone's—unknown generations hence. If you exist, I think it will mean that what I call the "Gatherers" have prevailed. Right now that seems unlikely.

There is so much worth salvaging; we have come so far. Yet, at the same time we seem to be devolving toward our own annihilation, wrecking the world around us in a final tantrum. No one with her eyes open can believe any longer in the inevitability of human progress.

It seems to me that what we've called "modern humanity" has been for so long engaged in a contest between two impulses: the impulse to gather (to draw close to something, to bring together in a body); and the impulse to hunt (to target for killing, wounding or capture).

I would hesitate to use these words with anyone in the present because the terms are so freighted with old meanings. But if you exist, you may be able to hear them differently with so much time having passed since their anthropological references.

For millennia, "hunters and gatherers" referred to the synchronous work of early humans to feed their own wandering bands. The hunters provided meat, the gatherers collected whatever nourishment the ground and foliage provided—bountiful or paltry. But I am saying, "please, if you exist, clear your mind of those historical definitions."

I will use "Gatherers" and "Hunters" as I've redefined them for myself, idiosyncratically, hoping they will speak to you.

If you exist, some one of you may be interested to know how the contest looked to one person now.

About the only thing I still believe in is that everything deserves to be understood, including everything human. To you, it may seem obtuse to stress that everything any person has ever done is human. But there have always been many who would like to circumscribe the word "human" in order to leave other people out.

If humanity still exists, it may mean you have gotten past such disdain for "the other." I want to say it *will* mean that you have gotten past this, for it is my unapologetic hope.

What I see as the impulse to gather is inclusive; the impulse to hunt, exclusive. The impulse to gather can be described with a gesture: a sweep of the hand that attempts to collect all those who have been left out.

The impulse to hunt takes aim instead, to separate, conquer or eradicate whatever may be defined by some group as less than human. With the future of the planet now so much in doubt, I think it's a rare person who does not, at least unconsciously, align hopes for the survival of this world with either gathering or hunting.

2

AFTER A GAP

IF YOU EXIST, AND HAVE JUST FINISHED the above, I should tell you that eleven years have passed since I wrote it. The Gatherers have proven so far to be too few in number. The Hunters thrive on their power; acceleration is their currency.

It appears to me that humanity is on a new trajectory. Public awareness of the changes has increased, but enlightened policy does not keep pace. Some hardly seem to have noticed.

What is still called "global warming" has been renamed

the "climate catastrophe" by those on the front lines. Hundreds of millions of refugees from war, drought, flood and famine have died or are sequestered in squalor on foreign soil. The "advance" (or wrong-headedness?) of genetic engineering pushes aggressively forward, as does the initial merging of the human with the mechanical and technological, with artificial intelligence and machine learning.

I am eleven years older, of course. I doubt that anyone my age expected to be facing her own mortality and the projected collapse of the web of life on earth at the same time. Accepting my mortality has been a long, though largely successful project. I don't want to die, but I hope for the right to choose when to end my own suffering.

Accepting the death of millions of species, perhaps including our own, is a more wrenching matter.

3

WHAT DOES IT MEAN?

WHAT DOES IT MEAN TO BE HUMAN?

This is the question we've asked ourselves through the ages. Have you stopped asking it altogether?

I will say that it saddens me that all the progress we have made toward intricate answers, all the clarity we've gained through social sciences, biology, psychology, history, literature and the passing of time itself is under threat even now by those who would shrug off the question as no longer useful.

What it means to be human is quite a different question

from "What is human nature?" for which we finally realize there can be no answer except to include what any human in any culture has done or felt.

For me, the question of what it means to be human is more pressing than ever, though my own answers reside in recollected incidents, not in academic definitions.

Here's such an incident . . . my young friend Olivia was only two years old, and I was holding the handle of her stroller while we waited for her mother to pick up food from a Mexican restaurant. We were looking into the window at the array of succulent plants. Something caught Olivia's eye. She pointed her index finger so insistently that it nearly bent back at the tip. Right in front of us was a large shriveled lobe on one of the plants. She whirled her head around to look plaintively into my eyes. "OUCH!" she said.

Her empathy for the apparent suffering of the plant struck my heart, and I leaned down to kiss the top of her head. Not a definition of what it means to be human, for some humans seem not to possess such empathy, this is only a glimpse at a quality I hold dear in humanity. For that matter, many animals besides ourselves feel empathy, something we've taken far too long to admit.

Do your children, your little ones, still imagine they know how other species feel? Do you still have little ones at all? Do you grow in number by sexual reproduction? Does it still take a long time for human progeny to mature? May I, in fact call you our "progeny"? Are we anything like each other?

Sometimes my own questions startle me, for they reveal my hope that most of the multi-faceted qualities of being human will survive the man-made manipulations already quietly manifesting.

There is a new divide between technologists and the rest of us. Meanwhile, the Gatherers and Hunters gather and hunt.

4

SEPARATION

I HAVE SEEN SORROW AND RAGE STREAM DOWN the
faces of Gatherers as they protest the treatment of migrants trying to cross forbidden borders between nations
too numerous to name.

I have seen Hunters with rigid mouths wrench scream-
ing toddlers from the arms of parents as they arrive from
Central America at our Mexican border.

I have seen split families ordered to wretched detain-
ment camps thousands of miles apart.

So cavalier was my government's attitude toward family

bonds that often there was not even a check box to indicate a child had been taken away.

When I say "I have seen" I mean only in documentaries, photographs, and other media. I cannot be everywhere for I'm far from being an omniscient author.

This is not science fiction or philosophy. It is like a note in a bottle set to sea in hopes of reaching you, if you exist in the future on some unfathomable shore. I will have to suppose that your superior abilities enable you to translate language of the twenty-first century into your idiom.

I have seen Hunters stop cars from Morocco at Spain's border. The engine is shut off; ECG stickers are placed on the hood. Like a stethoscope, the border guard's computer will pick up the beat of a refugee's heart in the undercarriage carved out by traffickers. Hunters pry apart a bumper to dislodge a body near death from its journey. They roll it onto the pavement.

I have heard a smuggler of migrants from Istanbul to Greece say, "The most important thing is the money. No one cares about people's lives. We fill boats fifty to sixty people over capacity."

And I have seen Gatherers thrashing through turbulent waters to save the few flailing survivors of capsized boats.

Do you still have border guards? Borders? Do you still have nations? I hope you have surpassed these things.

This blue jewel of a planet twirling in darkness has no artificial lines dividing it, except on maps drawn and revised by winners of war after war. For millennia, such lines have been made manifest by walls snaking across every type of terrain, rising first in wood and stone and now in steel and concrete crowned with rolls of razor wire, which glints when search lights illuminate desperate climbers fleeing violence and hunger, risking everything for a bearable life in a new land.

Did the generations between us, if I can call them that, learn to let humans and animals move, as all species on earth must do when conditions change?

Did they learn how quickly people can flourish when a new culture welcomes them?

Has the stranger been gathered in, or hunted down?

5

WHY "GATHERERS" AND "HUNTERS"?

W HY DO I OFFER UP THE ALLEGORICAL LABELS of "Gatherers" and "Hunters" to convey much of the conflict in our world?

To me, the words feel more supple and rooted in humanity than the oppositional concepts of "Good vs. Evil." Those are rigid and have misguided us through most of our history.

I don't believe there is an Evil force nor a Good one that directs human actions. Even if only unconsciously, "Evil" and "Good" are still tied to religious and supernatural beliefs, and are often the false distinctions through which we discriminate against others. Countless human psyches have been destroyed by guilt and fear of punishment which go along with "Good and Evil."

When I began, I told you there is only one thing that I still believe in—everything deserves to be understood, including everything human.

The brains of *Homo sapiens* are the most complex biological structures in the universe as far as we now know. If you exist, you might have something interesting to say about that.

I suggest there is so much we have yet to learn about ourselves beyond biology. I think each of us is an agglomeration of urges, waxing or waning at any moment. Even directly contradictory impulses are common to us all.

To me, Hunting and Gathering are opposing instincts which humans turn to when faced with social challenges. They also can be opposing passions which *cause* social challenges.

Throughout human history, there have been purely superficial differences such as size, skin tone, texture of hair. My hope is that, if you exist, there will have been so much intermingling, and therefore inter-breeding, that those superficial differences will have become immaterial to you. They make it too easy to break people into castes and to think in tribal terms.

Or it could be just as fine a solution if we maintained our distinguishing traits, but the Gathering instinct flourished and all variations were welcomed and celebrated equitably.

This seems to me the harder lift.

How I wish you could tell me which if either of these has been actualized.

Hunting focuses on differences, and so it spawns racism, the belief that all races are not equal in intelligence, talent or worth. Racism seems the most entrenched barrier to human cooperation.

When I spoke of the crisis of immigration and the plight of refugees, I did not think to mention, because it is so evident to anyone living in the present, that the desire to keep immigrants outside a nation's border is often based on skin color, even slightly different hues.

There are other differing characteristics which stir up the scorn of Hunters, but almost invariably the darker peoples are the ones who suffer. Using the trait of color as a measure of human worth seems so self-evidently absurd; surely you must have overcome this!

We come in all varieties of earth tones, yet even the labels we give ourselves and each other emphasize the extremes. Why? No one is actually "white" or "black." Do simplistic markers aid hunting?

6

A HISTORY COMPRESSED

I HAVE NO WAY TO KNOW HOW MUCH the subject of history matters to you. If indeed this note should ever reach you, the present era will be ancient history to you, and I am no historian.

I write this note as one individual to another based in part on things I have long known, in part on what is being uncovered or reinforced by the current collision of two events. That story, which I will get to soon, has a background of thousands of years . . .

For millennia, one human being was allowed to *own*

another. I hope this is shocking to you! The owner could make the other do his bidding, no matter how hard the toil, unreasonable the restrictions, brutal the punishments. This was called "slavery." It still exists in disguise, but I hope the practice in all its forms is nonexistent in your era.

I should mention, since I want always to be honest with you, that there are those currently predicting a dystopian future in which race and class struggle is only worsened by technological developments in what I've allowed myself to call our human progeny.

There will be time to talk with you about that difficult subject later.

Just as with refugees today, the pattern of slavery has always been that the darker skinned peoples were owned and abused by the lighter skinned. There were notable exceptions, such as in ancient Africa where emperors of dark nations owned dark slaves from different tribes. Slavery was never just about color, but about power and wealth.

All slave owning empires produced countless Hunters, who literally tracked down escaped slaves. This in fact was the origin of modern policing in the United States.

Today, prejudice and brutality by many police in the U.S. have outlived legal slavery by more than a hundred and fifty years.

Though there have always been Gatherers protesting it, police violence has been easy for most "whites" to ignore because they have almost never experienced it themselves, and have rarely witnessed it in their own neighborhoods.

The ruthlessness against brown and black people has grown more and more evident thanks to technology raising awareness among those who have been ignorant or numb. Now video of atrocious incidents can be captured on phone cameras so slender they slide into one's pocket.

Many acts of police killing unarmed black men and women have circulated around the world via the Internet. Outrage has been mounting, increasing the numbers of Gatherers. There are even Hunters beginning to open their minds. I should stress to you that I'm convinced no one is born a Hunter or Gatherer, and that neither quality has to be a permanent trait.

7

TWO EVENTS COLLIDE

Let me tell you a story that is unfolding in the world as I write. It is one that is giving hope to millions on every continent. I may have my heart broken again if the story fades, dies or twists even before I finish my note in a bottle to you. But because it makes my heart beat faster, I will tell it anyway.

A few months ago, just after I resumed my writing to you after the gap of eleven years, the first of two central events occurred—there erupted a novel pandemic.

Initially downplayed, it has already proven to be the worst in a hundred years.

So many are still suffering worldwide, with no end in sight. So many have died. With millions in quarantine, we have been largely isolated from each other. Though some have chosen denial, few of us no matter our color, have been denied basic information on the COVID-19 virus.

With half a million people, to date, having died horrific deaths, unable to breathe, subject to clots, strokes and organ failure, the hardest hit have been our elderly. Countless seniors quarantined from their dearest loved ones, have died alone. The lucky ones have had an exhausted, but compassionate nurse or caregiver in protective gear and vinyl gloves, to hold their hand.

There have been profound analyses of the staggering numbers of darker skinned people stricken by the virus. What we have learned confirms everything that black and brown humans among us have known and lived their whole lives, that systemic racism always puts them at a severe disadvantage. There are racial issues that, astonishingly, many whites still do not acknowledge or are recognizing for the first time.

Those of darker hues have died in much greater numbers from the pandemic. Is this because of some innate biological susceptibility? No, it's because of poor healthcare prior to the epidemic, because of poor access to medical help during the pandemic, because of poverty, unavailability of good nutritious food, because of front-line employment and numerous other systemic disadvantages.

Missing historical pieces are being filled in by scholars of every color, by people on the street not listened to before, and spokespeople for a group called "Black Lives Matter," which hundreds of thousands of us support. This is their time.

White minds were being sown with seeds of a new awakening just when the second, the pivotal event of the story, collided with the pandemic.

This second event was not so different in kind from videos capturing police killings in the last few years, not so different from a series of white on black murders by police that happened even in the most recent weeks.

But this was video from different angles, documented by citizens and police cameras alike, of the agonizing death by asphyxiation of a black man. His name was George Floyd.

It was a sadistic, casual killing by a nonchalant white officer, hand in his pocket, kneeling on Floyd's neck against the hard pavement. A second and third officer helped to hold Floyd down. The fourth did nothing to intervene in spite of spectators' outcries.

We heard the black man pleading for his life; we heard him gasp repeatedly "I can't breathe." We heard him call out "Mama!"

Now in dispute in seconds is the exact time it took, but for an eternity of at least eight minutes we watched Floyd's consciousness drain out of him. We watched George Floyd die.

Empathy often needs proximity to be activated. Millions worldwide, viewing the video of the callous murder of George Floyd, felt they were witnessing this atrocity in person.

Minorities in other nations recognized their own abuse in the chilling footage. In the weeks since then, millions have been in the streets protesting, most of us peacefully, most of us wearing masks to help protect from the pandemic. Yet we were making the choice that speaking up against murder and bigotry mattered even more than personal safety.

Many previously neutral or silent have joined the Gatherers pushing for change in ways at least as important as marching.

Protests have spread around the planet: in major world capitals like London, Paris, New York, of course, but more startling in metropolitan and small towns in South Korea, Columbia, Spain, Austria, Greece, Lithuania,

Germany, Pakistan, South Africa, Mexico, Netherlands, Germany, Italy, Syria, New Zealand, Austria, Sweden, Spain, Canada, Brazil.

Forgive my self-indulgence in subjecting you to such a long list of nations, but I could hardly help myself. It is not every day that I can feel pride in my species.

Still in lockdown from the pandemic, newspapers and radio stations provided interviews and documentaries earlier produced, which have been curated for their poignant relevance. Original productions are broadcast every day. The call for action, for real change in policing, for a focus instead on social services is loud and clear.

This is one of those rare thrusts forward when the best human qualities manifest themselves.

May it be a major turning point. If you exist, how I wish you could confirm that it was!

8

CATASTROPHE

W<small>E SAT ON A DEEP CONCRETE STEP</small>, she between my knees with the permanent curve of her upper spine nestled in my lap, and her wavy white hair against my chest.

We were resting after a labored walk from the front to the side of her nursing home, and she had deftly used her cane to lower herself into this perfect fit. We interlocked fingers on her stomach and reminisced about moments in the two years since we met and adhered like magnets when she was ninety; I was sixty.

We were looking up at a blue sky with lively clouds.

Her hyperawareness of the beauty of morphing skies was one of the best gifts she had shared with me.

"Isn't this *enough*?" she asked rhetorically. "Why do people think they need more, and more and more than *just this*?"

She was a Gatherer of the first order, a Jew who had worked all her life against prejudice of any sort. Referring to her eclectic collection of friends, she had boasted to me, "I pick up people all the time!"

Her regret at being ninety-two was that she could no longer march in demonstrations. If she were still alive and fit today, she would be marching for racial and climate justice.

If you exist, I wish I could see you and my friend through the same aperture just for a moment.

I keep wondering if our planet Earth is still your home as it has been ours. Given what we have done to ravage our only dwelling place, the "point of no return" as climate science calls it, is eerily near.

It might help if I lay down some of the present markers for you, who must know the outcome. I wish you could tell me how close we are, or how close we eventually will come to making this earth uninhabitable.

If indeed we go all the way, do you still exist somewhere—and if so how, and where? I hope that you will be alive and capable of answering, though I will never learn your response.

I could say to you that, "When we left Nature to her own devices, she was beautiful though she could be breathtakingly cruel. With human meddling, she's already become vastly more dramatic and vastly more ruthless."

But I don't want to say it that way because the concept of "Mother Nature" and so many other god-like personifications are counter-productive. They make us look away from the man-made changes we have created which thwart evolutionary adaptation.

Where are we on Earth's scientific timeline? At this point, how much time do most plants and creatures have left?

Here are some symptoms for you:

We are living in a hotter world, with a thickening coverlet of carbon dioxide which keeps the heat from escaping.

Long established animal and plant territories are deviating wildly.

It is impossible to calculate the numbers of species of plants, bacteria, insects, birds and mammals that go extinct on a day to day basis. Whole ecosystems have been destroyed.

Crops are failing.

Ice sheets and glaciers are melting so that ocean water expands, thereby flooding coastal towns and cities in nearly every country bordered by the sea.

But more frequent and heavier rain is causing inland flooding, too.

Horrific hurricanes, the kind which only used to strike about once every hundred years, now revisit some locations with such frequency that there's insufficient time to rebuild from the last.

In drier areas, droughts are as much a threat as flooding, and in some places forest fire seasons are beginning to last the year round. Even over media, it hurts to hear forest animals screech and scream as they burn to death.

In terms of humanity, the most vulnerable, those with the fewest resources and fewest choices, are suffering the most. Eight hundred million people now live in extreme poverty.

The rise in sea level could displace one hundred million humans. And our heartless treatment of refugees I have already recounted.

Migrations and conflicts over dwindling resources intensify the risk of more wars, and the propensity of the Hunters to conquer and subjugate.

How much longer, I wish you could tell me, did this go on? If you exist and are tiring of being on the receiving end of all my questions, you might wish to turn this one back to me, "What did all this have to do with Gatherers and Hunters?"

9

EVERYTHING

To MY MIND, THE STATE OF OUR PLANET has *every-thing* to do with Gathering and Hunting. I would hurry to add Hunting *more* than Gathering.

The ages before recorded human history account for most of *Homo sapiens'* existence. How superior those countless generations were in living in accord with the earth beneath their feet, just like today's rare remaining indigenous peoples who have not been colonial subjects.

If you exist and have some knowledge of ancient history, I ask again that you please dismiss any lingering associations, unlikely as they may be, with the anthropological phrase "hunters and gatherers."

In this note to you, Gatherers are simply those who seek to be inclusive. Hunters take aim; ultimately they eradicate.

It has not been long since I learned that the most critical damage humans have done to the earth has occurred within the blink of my own lifetime . This is a source of shame. It is also a spur to action, for I've learned from scientific reporting that with intense focus, determination and cooperation, the worst damage could be turned back within a single generation, beginning now!

We have the science, the creative brain power and most of the technology to accomplish this.

What we lack, maddeningly, is the will! The will, but also on many fronts the awareness, since so much has been done by those who hunt to hide the science from those who would gather.

Hunters have long believed that unlimited growth of industry, productivity, technology (read those words as "wealth") is required for human survival.

It makes no sense, as is true of so many beliefs humans take for granted. Has such an uncritical stance waned in generations closer to yours? That alone could make so much difference.

The planet Earth has limited resources. Rivalry over what remains of rain forests, of coal, of oil, of clean water is ripping humanity apart and causing extinction of the very people, animals and plants that Gatherers struggle to preserve.

Not all sources of energy are sustainable, and we have long known which ones are, for instance sun and wind. Pathetically, it is the burning of oil and gas and old growth forests, resources which cannot be replaced, that ruins Earth's atmosphere and bakes the planet.

Perhaps now you can understand how buoyed I felt when a tipping point was demonstrated recently in worldwide intolerance of racism: greater fairness in sharing limited resources bodes well for improved climate justice.

Did it take even more unimaginable death and destruction to mobilize a substantial majority of the Gatherers to convince enough Hunters to turn the tide? Oh, if only you could tell me that we came together in time!

If you were alive now and we were talking about the climate catastrophe, I would surely bring up the name "Greta", and you would know immediately whom I mean.

As I write this, Greta Thunberg is seventeen. In these few concentrated years since her childhood she has mobilized youth around the world to fight together for climate justice, in bitter recognition that adults have let them down.

Her awards and recognition as well as her public appearances before prestigious governmental bodies would impress anyone—anyone except Greta, herself.

She cares nothing for celebrity. Single-mindedly, she focuses on the goal she has set for herself and her generation—to act on behalf of the planet wherever adults have failed to act.

With soft blue eyes and penetrating gaze, she speaks in a sometimes unwavering, sometimes quavering voice, the truth from climate science that has been hidden. Her singular directness and even bluntness reach minds and hearts. She is a consummate Gatherer.

Recently I read in Greta's own words her conviction that her autism (Asperger's, a neurological syndrome) is her greatest strength. This was something I sensed from the first time I heard her speak. Perhaps a commonality with certain neurological disorders of my own drew me to be stirred to the quick by her ingenious use of her strengths.

Greta noted how adults perennially say, "leave it to the younger generation."

"How dare you!?" were Greta's words, trembling with passion, before the United Nations.

I agree. How dare we leave it to our children to climb the most insurmountable obstacles! It is an abdication of adult responsibility, an abandonment of our offspring.

Superficially, we look to youth for inspiration, but never cede real power to them over policy, though it is our young ones who will live or die amid ruins. If we don't lead with them and march next to them we will fail them and our planet.

For decades, many climate scientists have felt mortified, being mocked for their accurate modeling by wealthy Hunters taking aim at rain forests, at coal secreted under valleys and mountaintops and at oil beneath the corrugated skin of land and oceans. Despairing scientists, fearing that their dire predictions might set back their cause, have too frequently censored their own predictions.

It was not until the last few years that one freakish flood or fire or drought after another finally began to tear off the blindfolds imposed by powerful Hunters on public perceptions.

Seeing should be believing; experiencing, confirming.

10

IF THE CHILDREN
CAN'T SAVE US,
TECHNOLOGY WILL

Many who aren't ready to support our young people are perfectly prepared to believe that technology alone will save us. They are confident that humans will invent our way out of every predicament in the nick of time.

Because I hope for your existence, there is much more I yearn to say to you. It may be harder for me from here on because the subjects I've still not touched are even more convoluted and paradoxical.

Religious institutions have been ebbing for a very long time to different degrees in different parts of our world. Yet humans have always been compelled to adopt novel belief systems to replace the old, substituting new gods for long established ones.

Science and especially technology have become the new secular gods for those who have let go of supernatural explanations. Having these two new gods gives humans themselves a sense of almost supernatural power, the exultant feeling that we will be the creators of our own destiny and our own escape.

The scientific method has allowed us to grow in understanding of our world even though there are still those who endorse magical explanations. Some who endorse such explanations are cynical Hunters who take aim at the findings of science when they stand in the way of their profit.

Do individuals in your generation still simultaneously hold scientific and magical views? Or have you gotten past that?

Thanks to technology we hold in our hands what we call our digital "devices" *if* we are wealthy enough to own some. They enable us to communicate instantly around the world, to send images to others of ourselves and what we are seeing from moment to moment, to control household mechanics from afar, to direct robotic monitors in the medical realm.

These personal devices give humans a heady feeling about the present and future, and distract us from the problems for which no solution is in sight and none may be realizable.

Where technology and biology join forces, a number of prominent scientists have turned their backs on the future possibility of Earth as an inhabitable planet, and with it, the future of *Homo sapiens* as we have existed for millennia.

"Are these the cynics?" you might want to ask me.

No! These are the zealots! These are the "visionaries" who have turned their gaze from the problems right in front of us. They find it more alluring to anticipate the perfection of the human race beyond the flaws and limitations of *Homo sapiens*, and picture our perfected progeny and our *immortal* selves successfully colonizing other astronomical bodies throughout the universe.

11

REDESIGNING HUMANS

IF YOU EXIST, DO YOU CALL YOURSELF *Homo sapiens*?
Or has humanity so radically changed in the generations
upon generations between us that we are no longer the
same species?

"Why do you care?" I can imagine you wondering.
Can you detect how connected I've begun to feel toward
you that I imagine your questions whether or not you
exist?

I care because there are qualities of *Homo sapiens* that
I fear will be lost, replaced or warped if biology and

technology join forces to tamper with, or worse, permanently change what has resulted from slow evolutionary adaptation.

I care because, as I said early on, I believe everything human deserves to be understood. Instead of understanding, I worry that driving ambition and greed will lead to manipulation and eradication of valuable age-old human traits impossible to restore.

I would be naïve if I thought we could call a halt to genetic engineering. You may not know what I mean by "genetic engineering" even if you have moved past it to other forms of human redesign that I'm unable to imagine.

Our world has radically changed since scientists discovered individual genes are discrete segments of DNA, which contain the biological instructions that make each species unique and make each individual unique among its species. In reproduction, our DNA is passed from adult to offspring.

These have been valuable discoveries in our understanding of how evolution has worked throughout the ages. However, the issue of how and when to put genetic knowledge into action often has been a conundrum, and a temptation for *Homo sapiens*. Does it continue to be so for you?

All too often, we have been unable to resist plunging forward into the unknown for better or worse. I'm hardly the first to say we do things because we can.

But I don't believe I'm exaggerating if I tell you we have reached a dangerous precipice when it comes to biotechnology and genetic engineering.

I won't dispute that good things have come out of biotechnology. With a new surgical editing technique, biologists and medical doctors are able to substitute a faulty gene sequence with a perfect replacement. When precise genetic material in an individual's DNA is cut out, replaced, and the DNA rejoined, the result is introduced into the individual to change one or more of its characteristics.

This is where Gatherers must not become Hunters, taking aim at every improvement brought about by such methods. Gene therapy to treat or cure an individual of a disease or disorder from which many suffer is hard to argue against. Sadly, it also acts as a "foot in the door" for scenarios that people who believe in utopian futures have dreamt up, and are pushing like sacred revelations to those desperate to believe.

The power of gene therapy to "enhance," beyond curing *Homo sapiens*, is a subject of deep concern to me. Once a change is made to the "germ line" of an individual, that change will be passed along through eggs and sperm to future generations.

Likely, there will be no turning back.

Earlier I referred to a new divide between technologists and the rest of us. It saddens me that *Homo sapiens* have grown more and more specialized over the centuries to the point where the knowledge base of one specialty is incomprehensible to many or most in other specialties, much less to the average person.

Which people become technologists is not a matter of relative intelligence alone, but also a matter of opportunity and inclination. Most persons are trying to keep afloat just to feed their family, to stay employed and to process the amount of information (much of it false) that passes before their eyes and penetrates their ears on any given day, often with little time or education to sort it out.

How can we be expected to keep up with what the elite class of technologists and other specialists are dreaming up for our collective future?

Where does this leave us? If you exist, you might know how this led to whatever physical and cognitive form you now take. From my generation on, when critical decisions were made affecting the transmogrification or eradication of a species, animal or human, who made those decisions? Technologists communicating only with other technologists? Governments? Venture Capitalists? Gamblers? Politicians? Ideologues? Demagogues? I wish I could look backward through your eyes.

I don't mind confiding in you that writing this little section has not come naturally to me. I can add "technologist" to the list of descriptors that don't fit me, any more than "historian" or "philosopher." I am only an individual writing a note full of longing to you, an individual far in the future.

12

ACCELERATION

Since I've just written, "I wish I could look backward through your eyes," I realize I've fallen again into the trap of thinking I can imagine your form.

Faster. Faster! Is there no other clear, shared goal among human re-designers than speed? *Homo sapiens* seem so addicted to acceleration that we may soon expedite ourselves into an unforeseeable and undesirable species.

Let me imagine that, through scarcely believable serendipity, you come across my "note in a bottle" and are able to read it either by yourself or aided by some translation device.

May I ask you to look at the word "algorithm?" Is it still in common usage? It may not be, even if it turns out to have been the seed of your becoming. It means to us, a process or set of rules for calculation or other problem-solving operations, especially by a computer.

Since the contemporary adoption and adaptation of the word, the concept and application of "algorithm" have widened and deepened to the point where many or most bio-technologists believe that people are in essence very complex algorithms.

This does not depress these scientists. It spurs them on to further experimentation, for they already know how to work with computer algorithms.

Much of the medical world is going forward under the assumption that algorithms can replicate the processes of the brain. This conceptual leap has occurred so fast and quietly that it is completely unknown by most of humanity, or is seen by many as science fiction.

Though it is ignored or unseen by the political class, it may profoundly affect all of our progeny.

If it's possible, could you look at these words "Artificial Intelligence" and "Machine Learning"? These are predicted to advance the speed of human redesign exponentially.

Artificial Intelligence employs algorithms in ways analogous to human learning and decision making. Machine Learning uses algorithms that can be trained, and through experience, improve automatically. These algorithms eventually make decisions beyond the control or awareness of their original programmers.

Here I find myself in a ludicrous position, ignorant of what form you may take as a result of enhancement or as a result of continual evolutionary adaptation.

How I wish you could tell me whether your physical form is that of a naturally evolved *Homo sapiens* much more advanced than we; or of a cyborg whose artificial parts are inseparable from your biological ones. Or have you been engineered from inorganic substances?

Are you akin to a bodiless brain inside a computer, able to speak and respond very much like a human? Have you (your every thought and experience) been absorbed into the "cosmic flow of data"?

Homo sapiens have never been very good at prediction. However, we have a talent or need to imagine things that do not exist, and have even invented religions around our own inventions.

Much of the scientific establishment is swallowing whole a reverence for "Datism." Datists believe that the universe consists of the vastness of data, bits of information, in the form of data flows. They believe that advanced algorithms will know us inside and out. Because they will know what's best for us, they will therefore guide us as they will guide everything in the universe.

For those who crave the feeling of being part of something greater than themselves, this brings comfort, as does every other religion.

It's now 2020. Many scientists predict the year 2055 as the year in which the "singularity" will be attained, that is, the year in which artificial intelligence, aided by machine learning, will match human brain power and from that point on overtake *Homo sapiens.*

Whether *Homo sapiens* artificially morphs into a god-like being with eternal youth, ever expanding intelligence, and a collective memory bank; whether algorithms become the omniscient "angels" watching over us—wait! Just by writing about these prognostications in which I have no faith . . . *I feel I'm beginning to lose you.*

13

WHY DON'T WE USE
WHAT WE KNOW?

TURNING TO MEMORY...

I lift him dripping from the tub. The cooler air elicits a squeal and flurry of kicking as I rub my baby dry and cloak him in a hooded towel on my lap. He nuzzles for milk. My breast must feel warm against his chill cheeks. His whole body relaxes as he gulps and swallows.

In a few minutes I place him in his baby seat on the dining table where my friend is having lunch with me. She and I can hardly take our eyes off his enchanting, dancing limbs as we make small talk.

But now his eyes lock on mine. Something startling washes over his—a look of love so deep and unmistakable, mine can't help mirroring it and welling up.

I reach out my index finger for him to clasp.

"Oh Lillian, this feels so personal. I don't even know if I should be here," whispers my friend.

"Oh yes you should," I say, knowing that for these few moments nothing can break this mother child bond. How lovely to have a witness.

As a young adult my son occasionally wondered if he was too reserved. But he dislikes being predictable. No scripted responses for him! So he finds the most authentic, inventive or subtle ways to show his love and tenderness toward friends and family.

His intentional moment of eye contact, for instance, before we sign off from a video chat across the ocean contains a revelation of his core, a split-second flash of that first look of love. I was too young to guess it could last a lifetime.

Homo sapiens have learned so much about benign cycles, though we speak more often of vicious ones. Why don't we put to use what we know about raising our offspring?

That was rhetorical, of course. How could you know the answer no matter your form or content?

I have not held back my criticism of my species: the

way we shun the other; the way we treat animals as expendable and inferior, denying that we ourselves are animals to our core and that they, too, have intelligence and emotion; the way we ignore that plant species are all part of a delicate balance, the remains of which we must strive to preserve. But these egocentric traits are less those of Gatherers than Hunters.

For the sake of truth and empathy, we must never forget that there are no such distinctions when *Homo sapiens* come into this world. If you could hear newborn humans crying, each one for the same things: to be fed, to be held securely and lovingly, to have their hurts eased, to bridge the world of wakefulness to the world of sleep . . . you would agree that no one is born a Hunter or a Gatherer.

Is there a *Homo sapiens* baby who does not focus on her parent's eyes to teach her how to respond to everything that happens around her? There are few infants who do not learn to smile and then to laugh irresistibly, unwittingly rewarding his parents for weeks and months of sleeplessness.

Why would we artificially and permanently alter future generations when, over millennia, we have learned so much about ourselves which has allowed us to gradually mature and behave more consciously.

But too often parents impulsively, or out of a sense

of loyalty, parent just as they were parented without exploring the depth of accumulated human wisdom about bringing up children, though it is the most important subject affecting the future of our species.

There are little ones who do not have their urgent bodily and emotional needs met. Some become fragile adults. They may make it to young woman or manhood, but with constantly conflicted impulses tearing them apart.

Because of lack of love, or of abuse, or simply because of purposeful parental training they may lean toward hunting, aiming to hurt as they have been hurt.

Then circumstances, temporary or permanent, may cause them to circumscribe whom they see as fellow humans and what parts of this world are worthy of protection. They may be taught to aim for the elimination of others.

They may become Hunters through no fault of their own.

14

A COMMON STORY

Let me tell you a story which is more common than commonly recognized. It begins with young men and women who commit to serve their nation's armed forces, whatever that nation might be.

Why do they do it? Some out of obligation, some out of idealistic nationalism infused in them from their earliest years, some out of a need for education that they cannot pay for any other way, some out of a need to escape or a drive for adventure.

If they are called to war, the top of the hierarchy

forces these soldiers, most of whom are youngsters, to hone their hunting skills, even if they might have leaned toward gathering.

Every war sets back progress as Hunters become hardened and increase in number. I believe I have used the word "war" with you earlier in this note, but it's only occurred to me now (with a little leap of joy!) that it's a word which might not be in your lexicon if the subtle trend toward less warring continues. That is, if intervening generations have been allowed enough time to fully mature.

War is nearly as old as humanity, though was less common when wandering bands could avoid conflicts over resources by simply moving on. Since violence generates retaliation and more violence, the futility of war is that it settles nothing.

At the command of older men, war is set in motion, but fought for the most part by young men and increasingly young women—they who should have the greatest number of years ahead of them, the most to lose! I hope the outright injustice of this strikes your generation as it has many of us Gatherers who work against it.

15

HUMAN HUBRIS

W<small>HEN IT COMES TO</small> *HOMO SAPIENS'* <small>LUST</small> for speedy redesign, I will not deny, since my aim is to be honest with you, that I find the projects of "perfecting humanity" and "achieving immortality" to be full of hubris.

I wish you could tell me that these vain attempts were long ago abandoned, for to wish and dream of perfection and immortality is one thing. To tamper irrevocably with nature is another.

Yet behind the scenes in academia and laboratories, the risky projects of human redesign are being debated more and more earnestly so that it's becoming impossible to say whether our species will be content to remain *Homo sapiens.*

Gatherers are needed to hold the line, for the goals of Hunters, inclined toward tracking, excluding, and eradication could be applied in striving for the perfection they envision and the elimination of what they see as human flaws.

What "flaws" would they deem candidates for eradication? Surely most or all physical and mental "handicaps." I need only mention that autism might appear on some lists. That would eliminate my young hero Greta Thunberg who is one of the most inspired leaders in the current fight for our planet.

Going back only a few decades to Nazism, those with learning disabilities were sought out for eradication as imperfect representatives of the race. On a personal note, I might have been hunted down.

I look toward Gatherers to accomplish the ideal that every human deserves to be received with understanding.

16

THE PARADOX OF TIME AND RESTORATION OF PARTNERSHIP

It takes time and patient understanding to raise Gatherers. Yet the qualities of Gatherers about which I've been writing to you (empathy, compassion, inclusiveness, cooperation) are what we need to fully mature as a species.

We do not need to turn *Homo sapiens* into a more powerful, god-like species only to speed away from the planet we've ruined.

The craving for speed does not align with bringing up

new generations if we want hard earned wisdom to be passed along naturally. Our offspring are pressured too much as is.

But the passion for speed needs only to be redirected. From where does the urgency of time cry out? From the death throes of our planet. We have no time to delay in adhering to our scientists' and our youth's concerns.

Gatherers must learn to gather-in all possible Hunters to rescue our scorching planet. What better project to bring *Homo sapiens* together than for both Gatherers and Hunters to be laser focused on healing our common home; this includes the world's inequities, which are heightened by the climate crisis.

It is with a sense of humility and irony that I am about to do what I have asked you not to do, to think *for just a moment* of prehistoric "hunters and gatherers," if you know or can look up that history. Together, they formed synchronous societies. The skills of the original hunters, which included tactical tracking, trailing and taking discerning aim, deserve to be respectfully adopted. For their hunting was done to provide for the entire wandering band.

Those original hunting skills can be endorsed by present day Gatherers—not for killing—but in a cooperative effort to track and eliminate the man-made origins of the climate catastrophe, including the burning of fossil fuel and pollution of our oceans.

The contemporary paradox of time is that the cry of the planet for speed, and the cries of a child for patience are not at odds. We must cooperatively accelerate our pace in saving life on Earth while we deliberately raise the children of our own species with the empathic values of Gatherers, enhanced with some skills of the original hunters.

If you exist, how I wish you could assure me that this paradox was understood so that *Homo sapiens*, more mature than we, inhabit the recovered home we nearly destroyed.

17

IF WE COULD MEET

THESE LAST PAGES OF MY "NOTE IN A BOTTLE" must be, of course, the stuff of fairy tales, for we will never meet.

But allow me my fantasy, out of kindness.

I can imagine the world in which we meet. It is unquestionably the Earth on which I lived my days. I can see only my immediate surroundings so I can't glean how much more restoration you may need to do. But I know that I am home.

There are some creatures advancing toward me through

the trees, just as you do. Some of these animal species I have seen eons ago in North America, others only in photos. A few are completely unknown to me.

In their eyes is inquisitiveness, more about me than you. But there is no fear of either of us. They must not be hunted for food any more.

As you approach me, I perceive quickly, inexplicably, that you are more enlightened than I, which means you welcome me with no feeling of prejudice or superiority.

Your deep, unwavering gaze tells me that your enlightenment has emerged from the gradual maturity of generation following generation of Gatherers, not from the biotechnology of species-wide enhancement. That is, not from the artificial enhancement of your intelligence, memory and other cognitive skills, which would set us apart as two different species.

Perhaps that kind of species would be superior in the ways intelligence is sometimes measured, by speed in calculation and problem solving but at the expense of consciousness and mind-body integration. *Homo sapiens* think with both brain and body. The notion of a bodiless "brain" housed in a computer makes no sense to my senses.

I have some distinct differences in what I call my "mental wiring" which have sometimes prompted me to joke that I feel as if my brains are in my fingertips. The images and ideas I paint and write seem to spring full blown from my hands, often unseen beforehand in my mind's eye.

You put out your hands to me as a greeting, and as I extend mine, I notice one of yours is bionic, and I feel happy for you.

Human hands have always been an object of love and fascination for me. Your bionic one is beautifully designed and I am certain that long before now there has been two-way communication and sensation between your hand and brain as a result of human designed implants in both.

And this is fine, for I want individual humans to be healed and made as whole as possible without altering the germ line for our entire species.

In close proximity now, we communicate rather well with gesture alone. It is unsurprising but still gratifying, for in *Homo sapiens* gesture precedes language and often precedes even the understanding of concepts before they can be put into words.

With your beautiful tawny brown skin, you have a look of health about you, though not necessarily a look of perfect youth. I feel relieved that those obsessed with being perpetually young have not been allowed to forge ahead with a misguided search for immortality.

All *Homo sapiens* must die for our species to be refreshed by the next generations. It is a sadness we bear for the sake of humanity.

Homo sapiens are so social that we sometimes experience "skin hunger," the need for human touch. I do now, and apparently you do too, for when I open my arms you step into them and wrap yours around me.

I sink into your warmth. I sense that you are still largely flesh and bone and blood like me.

And I'm filled with tenderness for your precious mortality.

———

ACKNOWLEDGMENTS

My lifelong creative partner and filmmaking co-director and producer JP Somersaulter is always the first to read my writing. The fact that he knows me so well helps him to put his finger on what is working and what might be going awry in what I'm attempting to express. Along with his encouragement and faith in me, he manages to keep his perspective during all of the previewing and multiple readings of each work. I can never thank him enough.

Indispensable, too, has been my son Dave who was a helpful critic of my children's stories when he was a child, and has become an insightful editor of my books for adults as a professional writer himself. He and his partner Jen, also a writer, have generously shared their experiences in the publishing world.

Close creative friends have become editors, and professional editors have become friends over the decades of my writing career. I'm grateful to all of my draft readers: Janis Dees, Stephanie Hughes, Katy McCrone, Paula Moore, Marlayna Schoen, Bill Schubert, and my husband Michael, who has been beside me through every writing project in which I've become seriously involved.

When JP and I were making films, Michael was our "chief engineer," and now that I've turned to writing he is still giving of his time and creative input to guide me through every technical aspect of the changing world of publishing.

One of my favorite memories is of an evening when I was reading aloud to Michael for his always valuable feedback. Our dear dog Grommet was also listening attentively, cocking his head from side to side. He only cried when I stopped. What more could I ask for from a critic?

Mary Bisbee-Beek and Stephanie Hughes, colleagues and friends, have both opened doors for me in the past and present for which I'm sincerely grateful! Special thanks to two other close friends and former co-workers Susan Taylor and Pam Meiser for their unfailing support through the years.

I also want to acknowledge Sarah Miner, and others in the design department at Bookmobile in Minneapolis. They have been a pleasure to work with on the design of *IF YOU EXIST: In Search of a Reader Deep in the Future*, as they were with my previous book *9 FACES*.

INFLUENCES

Thanks to the following writers, researchers and documentarians for their influence on my thoughts and feelings recently and over time.

David Attenborough, documentaries including his witness statement: *A LIFE ON OUR PLANET*

Louis Cozolino, *THE NEUROSCIENCE OF HUMAN RELATIONSHIPS: Attachment and the Developing Social Brain*

Franklin Foer, *WORLD WITHOUT MIND: The Existential Threat of Big Tech*

Douglas P. Fry, *THE HUMAN POTENTIAL FOR PEACE: An Anthropological Challenge to Assumptions about War and Violence*

Richard Dawkins, *THE GREATEST SHOW ON EARTH: The Evidence for Evolution*

Michael Gazzaniga, *THE ETHICAL BRAIN*

Michael Gazzaniga, *HUMAN: The Science Behind What Makes Us Unique*

Susan Goldin-Meadow *HEARING GESTURE: How Our Hands Help Us Think*

John Gray, *STRAW DOGS: Thoughts on Humans and Other Animals*

Lt. Col. Dave Grossman, *ON KILLING: The Psychological Cost of Learning to Kill in War and Society*

Yuval Noah Harari, *HOMO DEUS: A Brief History of Tomorrow*

Yuval Noah Harari, *SAPIENS: A Brief History of Humankind*

Paul Hawken, *BLESSED UNREST: How the Largest Movement in the World Came Into Being and Why No One Saw It Coming*

Sarah Blaffer Hrdy, *MOTHERS AND OTHERS: The Evolutionary Origins of Mutual Understanding*

Marco Iacoboni, *MIRRORING PEOPLE: The New Science of How We Connect with Others*

Elizabeth Kolbert: *THE SIXTH EXTINCTION, An Unnatural History*

Thomas Lister, *MAN'S GREATEST FEAR: The Final Phase of Human Evolution*

Milène Larsson, *Vice News Documentary Series: EUROPE OR DIE*

Milène Larsson, documentary: *MAKE THE WORLD GRETA AGAIN*

Sue Mansfield, *THE GESTALTS OF WAR: An Inquiry into Its Origins and Meanings as a Social Institution*

Bill McKibben, *FALTER: Has the Human Game Begun to Play Itself Out*

Sherwin B Nuland, *HOW WE DIE: Reflections on Life's Final Chapter*

Loyal Rue, *NATURE IS ENOUGH: Religious Naturalism and the Meaning of Life*

Robert M. Sapolsky, *BEHAVE: The Biology of Humans at Our Best and Worst*

William H. Schubert, *LOVE, JUSTICE AND EDUCATION: John Dewey and the Utopians*

Gene Sharp, *WAGING NON-VIOLENT STRUGGLE: 20th Century Practice and 21st Century Potential*

Daniel J. Siegel, *THE DEVELOPING MIND: Toward a Neurobiology of Interpersonal Experience*

P. W. Singer, *WIRED FOR WAR: The Robotics Revolution and Conflict in the 21st Century*

Rebecca Solnit, *HOPE IN THE DARK: Untold Histories, Wild Possibilities*

Daniel N. Stern, *THE INTERPERSONAL WORLD OF THE INFANT: A View from Psychoanalysis and Developmental Psychology*

David Wallace-Wells, *THE UNINHABITABLE EARTH: Life after Warming*

Frans de Waal, *ARE WE SMART ENOUGH TO KNOW HOW SMART ANIMALS ARE?*

Franz de Waal, *THE AGE OF EMPATHY: Nature's Lessons for a Kinder Society*

Thomas G. West, *IN THE MIND'S EYE: Visual Thinkers, Gifted People with Learning Difficulties, Computer Images and the Ironies of Creativity*

D.W. Winnicott, *HOME IS WHERE WE START FROM: Essays by a Psychoanalyst*